THE
Fact Cat
PLANETS

Alice Harman

WAYLAND

FACT CAT

Get your paws on this fantastic new mega-series from Wayland!

Join our Fact Cat on a journey of fun learning about every subject under the sun!

First published in 2014 by Wayland
© Wayland 2014

Wayland
Hachette Children's Books
338 Euston Road
London NW1 3BH

Wayland Australia
Level 17/207 Kent Street
Sydney NSW 2000

Produced for Wayland by
White-Thomson Publishing Ltd
www.wtpub.co.uk
+44 (0) 843 208 7460

Editor: Alice Harman
Design: Rocket Design (East Anglia) Ltd
Fact Cat illustrations: Shutterstock/Julien Troneur
Other illustrations: Stefan Chabluk/Bill Donohue
Consultant: Kate Ruttle

A catalogue for this title is available from the British Library

ISBN: 978 0 7502 8222 2
eBook ISBN: 978 0 7502 8523 0

Dewey Number: 523.4-dc23

10 9 8 7 6 5 4 3 2 1

Wayland is a division of Hachette Children's Books,
an Hachette UK company.
www.hachette.co.uk

Printed and bound in China

Picture and illustration credits:
Chabluk, Stefan: 7, 11; Donohoe, William: 4-5;
NASA: 6, 9, 10, 12, 13, 14, 15, 16, 17, 18, 19, 20, 21, 22;
Shutterstock: Marcel Clemens 8, Maciej Sojka cover and title page

Every effort has been made to clear copyright.
Should there be any inadvertent omission,
please apply to the publisher for rectification.

FACT CAT FACT

There is a question for you to answer on each spread in this book. You can check your answers on page 24.

CONTENTS

OUR SOLAR SYSTEM

There are eight **planets** in Earth's solar system. A solar system is made up of planets that **orbit**, or move around, a **star**. The star in our solar system is the Sun. The Sun gives out light and heat.

The dotted line between Mars and Jupiter shows an area where there are many asteroids. These are small chunks of rock and **metal** that orbit the Sun.

Saturn

Uranus

Neptune

FACT CAT FACT

Until 2006, people said that there were nine planets in our solar system. The ninth planet was called Pluto, but this is now called a **dwarf planet** instead.

Sun

Earth

Mercury

Venus

Jupiter

Mars

Earth's moon

Apart from Earth, all these planets are named after ancient **Roman gods** and goddesses. Which planet is the only one named after a goddess?

Earth and five of the other planets have moons. These are large objects that are made of rock or ice. They orbit a planet, while that planet orbits the Sun.

MERCURY

Mercury is the closest planet to the Sun, so it can get extremely hot. However, the planet also cools down quickly. This means that it can be very cold at night.

So far, only one **spacecraft** has ever been to Mercury. Can you find out when it was there?

FACT CAT FACT

The **temperature** on Mercury can reach 430°C. This is more than seven times hotter than the highest temperature ever recorded on Earth!

Deep inside Mercury, there is a lot of iron. This metal is also found on Earth. We use iron to make buildings and machines.

Mercury is the smallest planet in the solar system. It is mostly made of metal. It has a thin **surface** layer of rock around its metal **core**.

VENUS

Venus is a much hotter planet than Mercury, even though it is further away from the Sun. This is because Venus has a thick layer of **carbon dioxide gas** around it. The gas traps the heat from the Sun.

There is more and more carbon dioxide gas around Earth, because of **pollution** from cars, aeroplanes and factories. How might this change the planet?

FACT CAT FACT

If you went to Venus, you would be squashed flat! This is because the air around you would be 92 times heavier than it is on Earth.

Venus is the closest planet to Earth, but humans could not survive there. As well as being far too hot, it also has no **liquid** water. The rain on Venus is strong **acid** that would badly burn your skin.

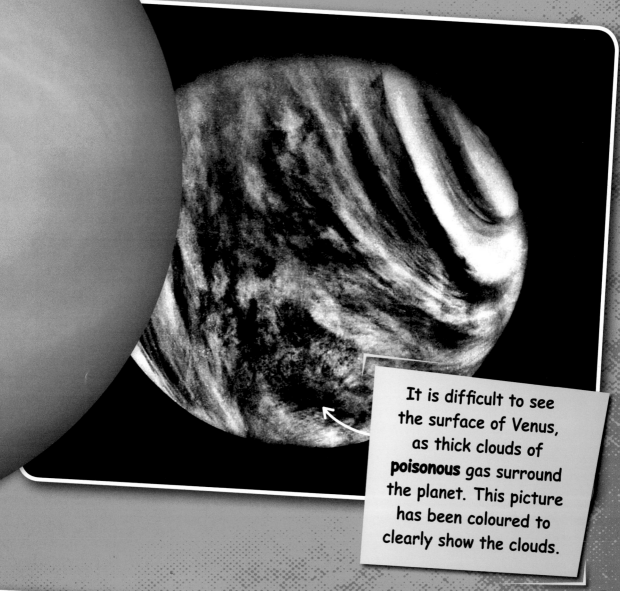

It is difficult to see the surface of Venus, as thick clouds of **poisonous** gas surround the planet. This picture has been coloured to clearly show the clouds.

EARTH

Animals and plants can survive on Earth because it is just the right **distance** from the Sun. This means it is neither too hot nor too cold for them. Most of the Earth's surface is covered in water, which almost all living things need.

Water in the ocean is salty. Humans and many other animals cannot drink salty water. Do you know what we call water that does not have salt in it?

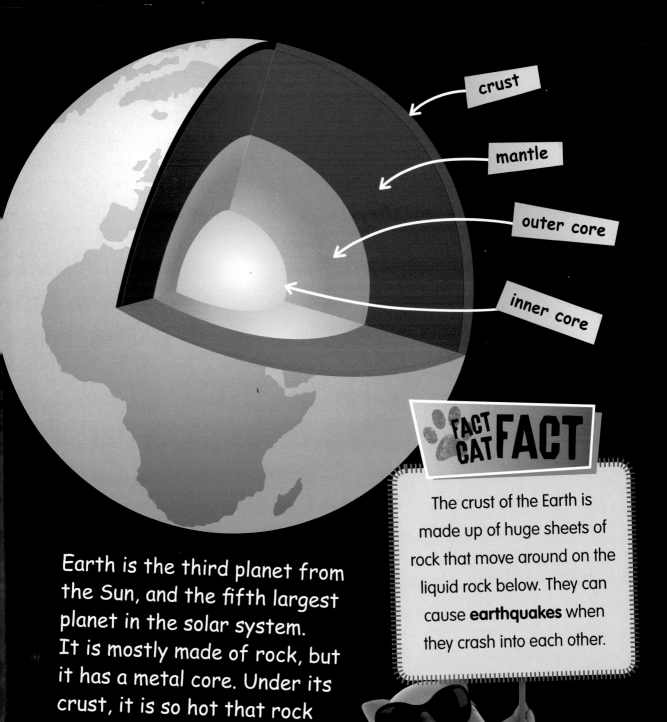

crust

mantle

outer core

inner core

The crust of the Earth is made up of huge sheets of rock that move around on the liquid rock below. They can cause **earthquakes** when they crash into each other.

Earth is the third planet from the Sun, and the fifth largest planet in the solar system. It is mostly made of rock, but it has a metal core. Under its crust, it is so hot that rock turns to liquid.

MARS

Mars is the planet that is most like Earth. It has **volcanoes**, **deserts** and areas of ice. However, Mars is much colder than Earth and has many more storms.

Mars is often called 'the red planet' because of its red-brown colour. What is the main colour of Earth?

FACT CAT FACT

Mars is about half the size of Earth, but the two planets have the same amount of dry land. This is because there is no liquid water on Mars.

Mars is the fourth planet from the Sun. It is the second closest planet to Earth. Several spacecraft and robots have been to Mars, but they have not found any living thing there.

In 2012, this robot landed on Mars to look for **evidence** of life. **Billions** of years ago, Mars was warm and wet enough for things to live there.

JUPITER

Jupiter is the biggest planet in our solar system. It is so huge that all the other seven planets could fit inside it at once. At least 67 moons circle around Jupiter.

Jupiter's four biggest moons were discovered more than 400 years ago by a scientist named Galileo. Can you find out the names of these four moons?

FACT CAT FACT

On Jupiter, there is a giant **hurricane** called the Great Red Spot. This storm is larger than Earth. It has been going on for at least 300 years.

A spacecraft called Voyager I took this image. It shows Jupiter's swirling gas clouds.

Jupiter is called a 'gas giant' because it is a huge planet that is made mostly of gas. It also has parts that are liquid. It does not have a **solid** surface like Earth does. It has a rocky core, but the rest of the planet is liquid and gas.

SATURN

Saturn is the sixth planet from the Sun. It is a gas giant like Jupiter, and it is the second largest planet in the solar system. More than 700 Earths could fit inside Saturn.

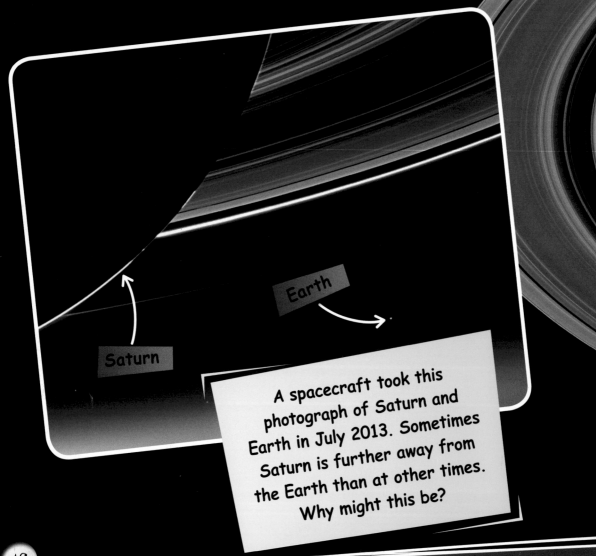

Saturn

Earth

A spacecraft took this photograph of Saturn and Earth in July 2013. Sometimes Saturn is further away from the Earth than at other times. Why might this be?

The rings in this picture have been brightly coloured so that you can clearly see them.

Saturn's rings are made of billions of pieces of ice, **dust** and rock. Some pieces are as small as a grain of sand, but others are as big as a house.

FACT CAT FACT

Saturn is the lightest planet for its size in the solar system. It is so light that it would **float** if dropped in water!

URANUS

Uranus is very far away from the Sun. This means that not much heat and light reaches this planet, so it is dark and very cold. Uranus is called an 'ice giant' because it is partly made of ice.

Uranus is the coldest planet in the solar system. It is 32 times colder than Earth. This photograph was taken by the spacecraft Voyager II.

FACT CAT FACT

Uranus is the only planet in our solar system that spins around on its side. Scientists think it may have been knocked over by another planet billions of years ago.

Uranus was the first planet to be discovered by someone using a **telescope** rather than just the human eye. The telescope was **invented** more than 400 years ago to help people see objects from far away.

This picture shows Uranus and its five biggest moons. Can you find out how many moons Uranus has?

NEPTUNE

Neptune moves very slowly around the Sun. It orbits the Sun once in the same time that Earth travels round the Sun 165 times. Since Neptune was discovered in 1840, it only has orbited the Sun once.

Neptune is very far away from Earth. Try to find out how long it took the spacecraft Voyager II to get near to Neptune.

Neptune has lots of extreme **weather**, such as violent storms. A telescope on Earth took this picture of some of Neptune's storms.

Storms

Neptune is a very cold planet. However, it is warmer than Uranus even though it is further from the Sun. This is because Neptune produces a lot of heat in its core.

FACT CAT FACT

Neptune is the windiest planet in the solar system. Stormy winds on Neptune can be ten times faster than hurricanes on Earth.

QUIZ Try to answer the questions below. Look back through the book to help you. Check your answers on page 24.

1 Which is the largest planet in our solar system?

a) Saturn
b) Jupiter
c) Mars

2 Which planet is closest to the Sun?

a) Venus
b) Earth
c) Mercury

3 Is Saturn the only planet that has rings around it?

a) yes
b) no

4 Which planet is shown in the picture?

a) Mars
b) Venus
c) Neptune

5 Which is the coldest planet in our solar system?

a) Uranus
b) Neptune
c) Jupiter

GLOSSARY

acid something that can burn materials that it touches

billion a thousand million (1,000,000,000)

carbon dioxide gas that contains carbon and oxygen

core part at the centre of a planet

desert hot, dry area

distance how far away something is

dust fine, dry powder

dwarf planet object that looks like a small planet but is not

earthquake sudden, strong shaking of the ground

evidence facts that show something is real

float stay on or near the top of a liquid

gas form of material that doesn't have a fixed shape or size, like air

god/goddess being that people believe has special powers

hurricane storm with very fast, strong wind

invent to discover how to make something

liquid form of material that can flow and that is wet, like water

metal material that is normally hard and shiny, like gold

orbit when an object in space moves in a curved path around another object

planet large object in space that moves around a star

poisonous describes something that will hurt you if it gets inside your body

pollution dirty, harmful substance such as smoke or car fumes

Roman to do with the ancient Romans, who lived more than 1500 years ago

solid form of material that you can normally see and touch, like rock

spacecraft vehicle, like an aeroplane, that is used to travel in space

star large object in space that is made of burning gas

surface the top layer of an object

telescope machine that uses pieces of glass or mirrors to make objects look closer

temperature how hot or cold something is

volcano hill with a hole in its centre that liquid rock can come up through from deep underground

weather changes in how hot or cold it is, and how much wind or rain there is

INDEX

ANSWERS

Pages 5-20

page 5: Venus is the only planet named after a goddess. Venus was the ancient Roman goddess of love. The other planets are named after the following gods: Mercury, the messenger god; Mars, god of war, Jupiter, king of the gods; Saturn, god of time; Uranus, god of the sky; Neptune, god of the sea.

page 6: 1974

page 8: It will make the Earth hotter.

page 10: fresh water

page 12: iron oxide, or rust

page 14: Io, Europa, Ganymede, Callisto

page 16: Because both Earth and Saturn orbit the Sun, so they are constantly moving.

page 19: Uranus has 27 known moons.

page 20: It took Voyager II twelve years to pass close to Neptune.

Quiz answers

1   b) Jupiter

2   c) Mercury

3   b) No. Jupiter, Saturn, Uranus and Neptune all have rings, although Neptune's rings are incomplete.

4   a) Mars

5   a) Uranus

OTHER TITLES IN THE FACT CAT SERIES...

UNITED KINGDOM

FACT CAT
ENGLAND
Alice Harman
9780750284332

FACT CAT
SCOTLAND
Alice Harman
9780750284394

FACT CAT
NORTHERN IRELAND
Alice Harman
9780750284400

FACT CAT
WALES
Alice Harman
9780750284387

COUNTRIES

FACT CAT
FRANCE
Alice Harman
9780750282123

FACT CAT
BRAZIL
Alice Harman
9780750282130

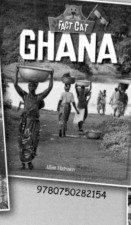

FACT CAT
GHANA
Alice Harman
9780750282154

FACT CAT
ITALY
Alice Harman
9780750282147

WAYLAND